Shutterbug Books
SOCIAL STUDIES

Many Kinds of Maps

by Susan Ring

STECK-VAUGHN

Harcourt Supplemental Publishers

www.steck-vaughn.com

There are all kinds of maps.
They are used for many different reasons.
Some maps help us find a place.

Other maps help us learn about nature.
Maps can also help us learn about countries or people.
Whenever we use maps, we learn more about our world.

Some people visit amusement parks on vacation. There are many exciting rides.

Th... ...usement parks are big places.
W... ...ow do people find their way around?
W...

On a nice day, some people like to hike in the woods. They stay on trails so they don't get lost.

There are many trails in the woods.
How do people know which trail to take?

Many people live in towns.
There are many buildings and streets in a town.

Most towns have parks where children can play.
How can people find out how to get to the park?

Big cities are full of people moving from place to place. Some people ride subway trains to travel quickly.

People get on and off the subway at a subway station. How do they know which trains to take?

At a stadium, people can watch a baseball game.
They might even see a great play up close!

This ~~sands~~ of people can sit in a stadium at one time.
Peo~~ple~~ do they all find their seats?
Wh~~at~~

Some people enjoy playing in the snow.
They like to go where the weather is cold.

Other people enjoy warmer weather.
How do they know what the weather will be like?

Some people like to climb mountains.
They use special tools to help them get to the top.

Climbers learn about the mountain before they start. How can they find out how tall it is?

The Earth looks very beautiful from space.
There are blue oceans, white clouds, and green land.

Pictures from space don't show country borders.
How do people know where the borders are?

There are many cities in the United States.
Some cities are very large, and some are smaller.

A huge number of people live and work in big cities. How can you find out which cities are the largest?

Each year, humpback whales make a long trip.
In the winter, they swim south to warmer water.

In the spring, the whales swim north again.
How far do the whales travel?

Every kind of map teaches us about the world. What can you learn from a map?